FATHER'S COMPASS

21 INSIGHTS TO GUIDE DADS THROUGH THE JOURNEY OF BUILDING A FAMILY

BY JEREMY PRYOR
FOREWORD BY JEFFERSON BETHKE

DEDICATION

To my one and only son Jackson: I'm so proud of the man you're becoming.

Raising you was one of the greatest privileges of my life.

Here's to our lifelong partnership and the house we're building together.

.

CONTENTS

ACKNOWLEDGMENTS

First, I'd like to thank the upstream relationships that have faithfully and skillfully helped me construct my father's compass.

- My Dad, Jerry Pryor: Your steadfast faithfulness has been like a beacon in my life, always guiding me to the Scriptures and our Heavenly Father.
- My Father-in-Law, Donald Seely: Your stories, your encouragement and the example you've set in the way you raised your daughter have guided me in ways you'll never know. We miss you and look forward to that largest of family reunions in our Father's Kingdom.
- My prayer warrior friend, David Sheldon: Your prayer over me is what finally released the writer in me.
- My father-coach, Mark Whitmore: The time, dedication, and love you showed to me by saying the necessary and hard things have healed both me and multiple relationships within my family. I'm so grateful for you!

Next, there are the horizontal relationships who have influenced and inspired my insights on fatherhood.

- My business/ministry partner and brother-in-Christ, Stephen Mowry: You've stuck by me through 20 years of seeking the Kingdom in so many diverse areas. Your loyal love for me has been a ballast and our deep conversations have helped me go so much deeper into these truths.
- My philosopher friend, Gavin Long: You always manage to make my vision of our Father's Kingdom bigger than I imagined.
- Our family teams partners, Jefferson and Alyssa Bethke: I'm so grateful for the miraculous way our Father drew us together. You make this work a joy everyday and we love you all!
- My constant encourager, Blake Smith: You always believed and boldly told me that I have something to say.
- My book editor, Adam Palmer: Once again you levelled up my writing. Thank you!

Finally I just want to thank my wife April and my five amazing kids, Kelsey, Jackson, Sydney, Elisa and Kaira. It's the greatest privilege of my life to get be your father and to get to lead this team. Never stop believing that we're better together.

FOREWORD

One of my first jobs was working as a server at Olive Garden when I was 18 years old.

If you've ever been a server, then you instantly know how interesting, difficult, and undervalued the job tends to be.

But also how quick and fast-paced it can be.

In fact, I still remember my training quite vividly: a full week set aside to learn the menus, hear about the company culture, and try every single dish on the menu (best day ever!). The knowledge was actually pretty in-depth, but at the end of the day we all knew that with the specific work of serving, you really just get your chops by actually serving.

It is quite a picture of on-the-job training. You can only learn so much beforehand; realistically, you learn most of what you really need to know once you already have the job!

It's fast. Stressful. High-octane. And you're making a thousand decisions on the fly at once.

But one saving grace? Those who have gone ahead of you. As a server you're a part of a team of others who have done the exact same thing and have probably run into the same roadblocks you will encounter. You can ask them for help. And I did! Over and over and over again.

I think fatherhood is a lot like that.

Or at least it should be.

It's on-the-job training. But you also shouldn't be doing it alone.

We were created to learn and be under fathers who have carved a path similar to the one where we want to go. Fathers who have families that are strong, healthy, vibrant, and full of purpose. We should hear from them. Listen to them. And ask them questions.

That's why I'm so excited about this book you're holding. Because it's exactly that. A shot in the arm of brilliant-yet-concise fatherhood insights. Ones that will make you think deeply and reflect greatly.

If you are reading this as a father, know this: you have what it takes. There is no greater joy or purpose than to step into God's design for you as a father coach of your family. And I hope this book encourages you as much as it has me.

Jefferson Bethke

01

THE FATHER PATH

Anyone on a complex journey needs a map.

Fatherhood is one of those complex journeys, a journey with multiple phases.

Here are my observations of what each stage tends to look like.

PHASE 1:

Putting Life in Order. A man learns to get up in the morning, put his pants on, keep his room clean, go to work, care for his hygiene, and resist falling into life-destroying addictions. As he grows in momentum down this path, this phase begins to overlap with the next.

PHASE 2:

Starting a Family. A woman of similar potential notices the momentum this man is making and they are attracted to one another. They fall in love, then make a promise to journey on this path together and have children. Now a man begins to learn the wisdom of shouldering responsibility, putting others first, caring for his health and modeling love and good behavior to his growing team. As momentum begins to build and the number on his team starts to grow, this phase begins to overlap with the next.

PHASE 3:

Building a House. Temporary housing that used to feel like freedom begins to feel cramped and unstable, but more than that this father's growing wisdom gives him a vision for the unique kind of family culture he wants for himself and his family. He wants those values reflected in his physical house. As he and his wife make a home that better reflects their unique family, the father tries to maximize the value he can give and receive for his work. As his skills mature, his income increases. He enfolds extended family and maybe even some friends into the circle of his leadership. A house becomes a household, and as momentum grows, this phase begins to overlap with the next.

PHASE 4:

Building a Community. The father can see his older children need more diverse influences and that problems just outside his household require a variety of skills and strategic alignment with other households to solve. These houses begin to join forces and accomplish things as a business, organization, church, or neighborhood that he could never hope to accomplish on his own. As this community gains momentum, this phase begins to overlap with the final phase.

PHASE 5:

Ruling a City. Imagining the blessing it would be to see hundreds or thousands of others take shade under the flourishing order the father has shepherded in the previous four phases, he stretches out to launch the largest possible entity that spreads his values over the greatest number of people wanting to live within the sphere of his vision. This might look like a large business, a group of businesses, an expanding church, a network of churches, a village, or an actual city.

One of the most vivid examples of someone captured by the path of the father was Walt Disney. Toward the end of his life, his co-workers noticed he constantly carried around a small book called Garden Cities of Tomorrow. Shortly afterward, Disney fell ill and, on his deathbed, had a map of the city he had architected taped to the ceiling of his hospital room in order to try and complete his life's work which had culminated in this moment.

Every year I go to Florida just to walk around inside his final vision, which is best reflected not in the theme parks of Disney World, but the over $1 billion city built on his vision called Celebration, FL. Last week I spent several days in his city and was inspired by a father who made it so far down the fatherhood path.

Some fathers neglect the responsibility of taking the father path, while others seek to skip steps along the way. As Jordan Peterson wrote, "If you cannot bring peace to your own household, how dare you try to rule a city." These phases exist for a reason; we need to gain wisdom and maturity from each before moving on. We know our destiny is to rule cities.

"'Well done!' the king exclaimed. 'You are a good servant. You have been faithful with the little I entrusted to you, so you will be governor of ten cities as your reward.'" (Luke 19:17)

Isaiah, perhaps the Old Testament prophet who peered furthest and deepest into the future, described what's coming by saying,

"Behold, a king will reign in righteousness,
  and princes will rule in justice.
Each will be like a hiding place from the wind,
  a shelter from the storm,
like streams of water in a dry place,
  like the shade of a great rock in a weary land." (Isaiah 32:1-2)

So, men, let's do what we can to walk down the path. Let's put our room, house, household, and community in order so that we may learn the skills we're going to need to become wise and loving rulers in our Father's Kingdom.

02

WHAT AM I SUPPOSED TO DO WITH A NEWBORN?

Virtually every modern Western man who has just welcomed a baby asks the same question:

"What are you supposed to do with it?"

Many start losing interest almost immediately, while the more persistent among us poke, swing, throw, or scare the baby in an attempt to get some kind of reaction.

But even if the baby rewards these efforts with a startled look that makes us laugh or an occasional smile that warms our heart, we can't help but wonder if these rather meager offerings are worth the enormous sacrifice this kid is costing us.

But what if we're asking the wrong question?

Perhaps we should take a step back, and instead of asking "What am I supposed to do with it?" ask "What is it"?

We think we know what it is—it's a baby. But that's not good enough. Because families today have fallen so far from their original design we don't know what a baby represents or what a baby means. So we find some other category we do know and put it into that.

Some talk about their baby primarily as a biological life form: "All it does is poop and sleep."

Some think about their baby as an annoying duty: "I can't believe it wakes me up at night!"

Others see it as a pet: "Look it can roll over now."

While others dress it up as a kind of mascot: "Have you seen her new jammies with the bunny ears?" or "Check out his new mohawk!" But I've noticed the best, most attentive dads in our culture tend to put the child into the category closest to our Western, individualistic hearts, the toy: "Watch how she sucks on my nose."

I've said and felt all the things above, and having these thoughts or feelings is not bad. It's very normal, but I realized I was doing these things in a desperate attempt to carve out a place in my heart for

this newborn.
But I've learned something after having five kids and making many different attempts at this.

There was already a place in my heart for my kids! I just needed to find it.

God actually made every human being with a place for each kind of family relationship: father, mother, son, daughter, brother and sister.

Because family has been degraded, those places are buried deep inside and can be difficult to find. But we must find those places and not simply settle for one of the more familiar categories above, because when we do, our relationship with our child tends to continue inside that category, shaping our future relationship with them.

They need to sense they are a son or daughter, not a pet or a toy. And that starts with you bringing them into that place in your heart. So how is this done?

STEP #1:

Learn what a son or daughter really is. Scour the Bible and see what sonship was by looking at how Abraham felt about Isaac, how David felt about his sons, and how the Father felt about Jesus. Look at how Ruth played the role of daughter. Read great ancient stories (especially myths and legends) when people still remembered what a son or a daughter really meant.

STEP #2:

When God gives you a son or a daughter, *call* them son or daughter in your heart. When you hold them, say "my son" or "my daughter" over and over. Open yourself to the feelings that will emerge. I believe this is a major reason we're given an entire year to just hold our helpless little newborns, so that we have time to bring them into our core.

STEP #3:

Allow them to change your identity. The identities *son* or *daughter* only exist to the extent that the identity of *father* or *mother* exist. In other words, if you resist deeply taking on the identity of father or mother, your child will also struggle connecting to their identity as a son or daughter. For dads, this means actually thinking of yourself *primarily* as a father. What does it mean to live each part of your life as a father? Father is the only identity big enough to provide a framework for your work identity (i.e. now you work to provide for your family) your husband identity, and your masculine identity at the same time. Yes, you can still have other identities, but this one is really big. Embrace it.

STEP #4:

Repeat the above three steps with each child.

The result will be dramatic, and your children will actually be different children even at a very young age. A child that senses their father appraises their worth based on how much they can amuse their dad (the toy identity) will become a very different kind of kid than a child who knows they've captured the deepest place in their father's heart.

03

THE ROOT PROBLEM OF FATHERLESS-NESS

There is a concerted agenda in the media to avoid talking about fatherlessness as the root cause of many of society's problems. Discussing fatherlessness risks telling men they need to sacrifice their freedom for their families and risks telling women they may need a man in order to have a healthy family life. Freedom to men with no strings attached and more independent power to women are idols so sacred to our current culture that any facts or issues that might threaten their ascendance represent modern heresies that must be silenced. But the impact of these doctrines has been devastating to children, especially boys.

In 2018, psychologist Warren Farrell, historically a leading champion for expanding women's rights for decades, published a bombshell book called *The Boy Crisis*. Farrell, a long-time Board member for the National Organization of Women (NOW) resigned after it became clear these leaders of the women's movement were willing to suppress inconvenient facts that might help children if publicizing them might constrain their vision of freeing women from all responsibility.

Farrell turned his attention to studying the root causes for why boys are struggling. He points out that in every one of the largest 70 developed nations, boys have fallen behind girls, and what they have in common, Farrell says, is the dad-deprivation that comes from divorce.

He discusses this in detail in his chapter on Dad-Deprived Boys vs. Dad-Enriched Boys. And let me pause for a moment and let this sink in. It is now necessary to create a new category called the "Dad-Enriched Boy".

Farrell writes:

"These boys will also be more likely to have low self esteem, fewer friends, be depressed, have nightmares, talk back, be disobedient, and are likely to do worse in every single academic area, especially reading and writing, and math's and science."

"These boys hurt: and boys who hurt, hurt us – and themselves." He refers to prisons as "centers for dad-deprived boys" and notes the 700% increase in incarceration since the 1970s.

As an example of the pain of fatherlessness, Farrell mentioned Anthony Sims, known as the Oakland Killer. His last Facebook post was this: "I wish I had a father."

Farrell observes, "Whenever only one sex wins, both sexes lose." For every girl who turns out well, she'll have a boyfriend or son whose issues she must deal with. Even if you do not have children, you are paying for the boy crisis in taxes: boys on welfare, in prison, unemployed, joining violent identity-related movements, doing school shootings, etc.

Farrell believes the gap between dad-deprived boys and dad-enriched boys will become the single biggest predictor of those who become economically poor versus economically rich. Yet when discussions of wealth inequality come up, you just never hear about fatherlessness even being one of the causes...I wonder why?

The data shows that, when the lack of a father is controlled for, a lower income can be more than compensated for by the presence of a father.

How can this be?

Let's consider one of Farrell's examples: the father's role in creating delayed gratification.
Dads tend to build bonds with their sons by, for example, playing games and rough-housing, and then use the resulting bond as leverage for their sons to "get to bed on time" lest there be "no playing tomorrow night."

This boundary enforcement teaches boys postponed gratification, whereas boys with minimal or no father involvement are more frequently addicted to immediate gratification. Additionally, having minimal or no father involvement increases the chances of video game addiction, ADHD, bad grades, less empathy, less assertiveness, more aggression, fewer social skills, more alienation and loneliness, more obesity, anger, drugs, drinking, delinquency, disobedience, depression, suicide, and prison.

We must choose to not join the conspiracy of silence around the root cause of so many of society's problems: fatherlessness.

Albert Einstein once said, "If I had only one hour to save the world,

I would spend fifty-five minutes defining the problem, and only five minutes finding the solution." A culture refusing to identify the problem will never find a solution. So, for now, the problem will continue to grow.

So dads, in the face of these realities, never doubt how critical you are to your sons. Your loving presence in the home, guiding and disciplining your sons, is doing more than you will ever know to shape their future and the future of our society as a whole.

04

THE PREDICT- ABLE TRAP OF A PEERCEN- TERED CHILD- HOOD

There are so many ways kids today are growing up in environments never before attempted or, in many cases, even imagined. One of these social experiments we've been running both in the church and at school is to raise and educate kids almost entirely in same-age groups. It's clear the advantages to this system for both control and for curriculum. The transition from the one-room schoolhouse to same-age classes emerged from the need to educate children at a massive industrial scale.

This, in turn, has given rise to a new kind of person: the peer-centered child. We now tend to take it for granted that a child will care less about their parents' opinions of them and more about their peers'. We assume, because this is so common, this is healthy socialization. But is it?

After spending decades looking at the data, two secular Canadian doctors are now claiming this development is extremely unhealthy and even dangerous. In their ground-breaking book, *Hold Onto Your Kids, Why Parents Need to Matter More than Peers* they lay out this thesis: "Children today look to their peers for direction—their values, identity, and codes of behavior. This 'peer orientation' undermines family cohesion, interferes with healthy development, and fosters a hostile and sexualized youth culture. Children end up becoming overly conformist, desensitized, and alienated, and being 'cool' matters more to them than anything else."

Their prescription? Increase parental influence and reestablish proper hierarchy in the home in order to make our kids feel safe and understood, and earn back their loyalty and love.

I find this kind of language fascinating. One reviewer of the book on Amazon summed up the author's stories: "Like countless other parents, Canadian doctors Neufeld and Maté woke up one day to find that their children had become secretive and unreachable. Pining for time with friends, they recoiled or grew hostile around adults. Why? The problem, lies in a long-established, though questionable, belief that the earliest possible mastery of the rules of social acceptance leads to success... Multiple playdates, daycare, preschool and after school activities groom children to transfer their attachment needs from adults to their peers. They become what the authors call 'peer-oriented.'"

Again from their book: "Peer-oriented children are obsessed with who likes whom, who prefers whom, who wants to be with whom. There is no room for missteps, for perceived disloyalty, disagreement, differences, or noncompliance. True individuality is crushed by the need to maintain the relationship at all costs. Yet no matter how hard the child works, when peers replace parents the sense of insecurity can escalate until it is too much to endure. That is often when the numbness sets in, the defensive shutdown occurs and the children no longer appear vulnerable. They become emotionally frozen by the need to defend themselves against the pain of loss, even before it actually occurs."

"Our failure to keep our children attached to us and to the other adults responsible for them has not only taken away their shields but put a sword in the hands of their peers. When peers replace parents, children lose their vital protection against the thoughtlessness of others. The vulnerability of a child in such circumstances can easily be overwhelming. The resulting pain is more than many children can bear. Studies have been unequivocal in their findings that the best protection for a child, even through adolescence, is a strong attachment with an adult."

The Bible illustrates the danger of this orientation through a story that occurred more than 3000 years ago. One of the greatest tragedies, the division of Israel into the southern and northern Kingdoms was the result of a young, peer-oriented King. Solomon's son Rehoboam was given sage advice from his father's counselors but instead turned to the buddies he grew up with to set a policy that would determine the fate of the Kingdom. After the people implored the new King for mercy, we read in 1 Kings 12:13-14, "And the king answered the people harshly, and forsaking the counsel that the old men had given him, he spoke to them according to the counsel of the young men, saying, 'My father made your yoke heavy, but I will add to your yoke. My father disciplined you with whips, but I will discipline you with scorpions.'"

An avid example of what his father Solomon wrote to him in the book of Proverbs ("He who walks with wise men will be wise, but the companion of fools will suffer harm."), this one act of foolishness cost Rehoboam more than half of his Kingdom.

When we seek to build multigenerational families, our children must have both the skill to interact intergenerationally and the experience of deep and enduring attachment to their parents throughout their childhood. Forcing our kids to spend a huge percentage of their childhood in same-age groups without the engagement or protection of their parents or family will predictably give rise to this intractable peer orientation.

Our entire society is designed around breaking up the children of the family into these same-age groups from sports to schools and even to church programs. Creating alternatives to counter this pattern is challenging and costly to the family but perhaps not as challenging or costly in the long-term as losing the hearts of our kids.

05

THE HOPE IN FATHERING A FAMILY

We had a few newly married couples over recently, and they asked each person in our family to share what we like most about family. I was surprised by the answer that entered my heart as I pondered their question. One thing I like most about family is that family gives me hope. Watching my family grow in health and love is such a tangible way to "see the goodness of the Lord in the land of the living." (Psalm 27:3).

My favorite description of the goodness that comes from family is from Psalm 128.

Take a minute and consider why this psalmist feels so blessed by his family life.

"Blessed is everyone who fears the Lord,
  who walks in his ways!
You shall eat the fruit of the labor of your hands;
  you shall be blessed, and it shall be well with you.
Your wife will be like a fruitful vine
  within your house;
your children will be like olive shoots
  around your table.
Behold, thus shall the man be blessed
  who fears the Lord.
The Lord bless you from Zion!
  May you see the prosperity of Jerusalem
  all the days of your life!
May you see your children's children!
  Peace be upon Israel!"

Another title we could use for Psalm 128 could simply be, "The Good Life".

Consider the elements that for this psalmist made up the good life. Things like:

- Your wife as a fruitful vine within your house
- Your children like olive shoots around your table
- Living to see your children's children
- Living to see the prosperity of Jerusalem

Thus is the man who is blessed by the Lord.

Here's an exercise that illustrates the story you feel encapsulates the good life. Draw a single line that represents your life, from the time you were born to a point when you're about 80 years old. As you draw, make the line go up when you think you're experiencing the good life and down when you think you will be enjoying life the least.

Take a step back and look at that line.

We have a strange idea in our culture that the pinnacle of life is the college years when we still have our youth and before we take on too much responsibility. In fact, at my graduation party from high school someone told me to enjoy the next few years because, from his experience as an older man, he can say those are likely to be the best years of my entire life.

For so many in our culture, our lines peak in our early or mid-20s. But Psalm 128 really shows a steady line up and to the right, indicating the true pinnacle of life is at the end of it, when we're grandparents who have lived to see our children's children.

Scripture describes peak as a grandfather surrounded by his grandchildren in the latter years of his life. For the father who fears the Lord, has a fruitful wife, invests in his kids, and lives wisely is building toward that pinnacle.

What a different world we would have if every man had that vision for his future! How much better this world would be for women and children. This is the real problem with society: short-sighted men desperately lurching for happiness and hope but feeling incapable of finding it because they don't have their compass pointed toward the blessed life.

I get to witness this peak experience firsthand at our weekly Shabbat. Virtually every week, April's dad would hear something a grandchild would say or experience the closeness or meaning of family through some discussion and he would begin to tear up. He felt this blessing. Watching his eyes well up with tears showed me that his heart just couldn't contain the meaning he was experiencing in that moment.

"Behold, thus is the man who is blessed by the Lord."

So to all you dads out there, overwhelmed by financial pressures, the physical demands of little kids, struggling to find intimacy with your wife, feeling alone and wondering if it's all worth it, I say, "Hold on, brother." Don't throw in the towel. Find the wonder and meaning and blessing on the other side of the struggle. It's not easy—it was never meant to be. But if you persevere and build your house, then you will experience the blessing the Lord wants for each one of us fathers. Don't despair. Don't give into doubt. Have hope.

06

THE FATHER-HOOD SNOW-BALL

Dave Ramsey, the famous financial advisor to families in debt, emphasizes a technique he has helped popularize called "the debt snowball." It involves listing all your non-mortgage debt from smallest to largest and focusing all your attention on the smallest debts in order to gain a sense of momentum, like a snowball growing as it rolls down a hill. You're going to need that momentum for the hard months and years when you slam into your bigger debts.

Most financial advisors would recommend paying off debts of highest interest first but this idea of prioritizing momentum is often the under-considered element when you need to sustain hard work over a long period of time.

Fatherhood, like debt, is also hard work over a long period of time. So where do you start in order to gain the momentum needed to take on a growing list of responsibilities?

More kids are coming, along with more activities, the teenage years, seasons of tension in your marriage.

When you see these kinds of challenges you'll inevitably face as a father, where is the best place to start in order to build momentum? There's one place you need to master early, a place that tends to make everything harder or easier down the road, and it's one that many fathers have a fair amount of control over in the early years of the family.

That place is your work.

The decision of what kind of work you choose, where you choose to work, and how you choose to progress in your career plays an enormous role in whether you gain the proper momentum to build a multigenerational team on mission.

Work can provide the money, time, energy, and flexibility to help you manage the coming challenges or it can constantly get in your way. These challenges are predictable, and tackling them first in order to gain momentum will be immeasurably helpful in the years to come.

And this is why Solomon gave this sage advice to his son in Proverbs 24:27: "Put your outdoor work in order and get your fields ready; after that, build your house." Establishing stable and sustainable streams must be prioritized first.

Often I find fathers whose job works against their goals for their family. They were asked throughout their school years, "What do you want to be when you grow up?" This question makes work sound both like their main identity (what do you want to be?) and a decision that is entirely based on their individual wants (what do *you want?*). Most fathers have never asked the question this way: given my skills and passions, what kind of job would best provide for my family team?

As you desire to see your house scale up in both size and fruitfulness, you need a field that can cooperate. A career path that is guaranteed to require more of your time the older you get, at the same time your family needs more of your time, may force trade-offs you don't want to make.

On the other hand, having a field where your work in the early years yields a return later when your family needs your presence or leadership most can provide the needed momentum to tackle the challenges of a growing, expanding household.

Build off the momentum created by establishing your field so that when you most need it, your field can feed your family.

07

THE SAFETY IN RAISING DANGEROUS SONS

Here's an ancient idea that seems out of step with current cultural trends: if you seek to build a lasting family line and are blessed with a son, make it your goal to train that son to be dangerous. Give him the psychological and physical skills to withstand the assaults of other strong men.

There was a time when this was obvious, when family survival depended on raising strong sons, but in our recent drive to enforce equality between the sexes there is a not-too-subtle campaign to make men weak. This is not helpful when building multigenerational families.

Of course we must be careful with this line of thinking, because we know a dangerous son raised without an even stronger man to shape his growing strength can be a danger to his own family and to others. But with an involved father or male role model channeling and training a son's growing strength, these boys will make their families and the world safer.

Wait, you might ask, *I thought we were supposed to be meek?* The idea of meekness was most famously taught by Jesus in the Sermon on the Mount when He said, "The meek share inherit the earth." What exactly is the meaning of the word *meek?* The dictionary definition is "quiet, gentle, and easily imposed on" which seems to indicate someone who is spineless.

This can be seen as the opposite of the strength I'm describing, but the English word *meek* has changed over the centuries. This is one of those cases where it's helpful to look at the original word used in this passage and I was surprised to discover the word we translate *meek, praus* (prah-oos) in Greek, is actually a military word. Sam Whatley describes how it was originally used:

> The Greek word "praus" (prah-oos) was used to define a horse trained for battle. Wild stallions were brought down from the mountains and broken for riding. Some were used to pull wagons, some were raced, and the best were trained for warfare. They retained their fierce spirit, courage, and power, but were disciplined to respond to the slightest nudge or pressure of the rider's leg. They could gallop into battle at 35 miles per hour and come to a sliding stop at a word. They were not frightened by arrows, spears, or torches. Then they were said to be meeked...unflinching in

the presence of danger. Some war horses dove from ravines into rivers in pursuit of their quarry.. These stallions became submissive, but certainly not spineless. They embodied power under control, strength with forbearance.

Another concept that describes *praus* was having a sword and knowing how to use it but choosing to keep it sheathed. This was the *meekness* embodied by Jesus, who had an army of a hundred million angelic beings waiting for a single word while He chose to be mocked, tortured, and killed for you and me. That is the kind of strength we need to cultivate in our sons, but it starts with them being made strong instead of weak. They must possess a sense of power while voluntarily channeling that power to the service of the most vulnerable members of society, their family, and their Father's Kingdom.

We live in a fallen world, and our children and our families in the future will face threats and challenges impossible for us to foresee. To confront these dangers and to provide safety and stability for our families in the future, we must raise up dangerous sons. But not the overly-aggressive, cocky, or proud boys who are looking for a victim to prove to themselves they are strong. We must raise men of power whose strength and training have been cultivated by fathers, grandfathers, and mentors to make safe the city of God. Raise your sons to be so dangerous and so meek that, God willing, no one will feel it is safe to test their strength.

08

THE FAMILY VS. MISSION DILEMMA

Christian parents are watching their kids leave their faith at alarming rates. Recent statistics suggest that close to 80% of kids who grow up in evangelical Christian homes will abandon the beliefs of their parents. And kids of Christian pastors and missionaries are often no exception.

A figure that often emerges in this discussion is the late evangelist Billy Graham. Perhaps the most revered leader in the evangelical world in the 20th century, Billy Graham lived an extraordinary life and was famously disciplined about living out his convictions, which is why many of us scratch our heads when we learn that he would leave his family for up to six months at a time. This was no accidental oversight on his part. Many Christian leaders of his era believed prioritizing the mission over family was simply a part of following Christ; even Jesus made many strong statements about following Him at a cost to one's family.

Billy Graham and his wife Ruth embraced this missionary lifestyle as part of their calling. Their son Franklin speaks of not recognizing his father when he came home, and Graham himself related a time when he saw a little girl playing in a field and didn't find out until later that she was his own daughter. Sermons on the importance of parenting and ministries that encourage us to focus on the family have tried to address this problem but they seem to often misdiagnose its root.

We are story-formed creatures, and as committed Christians we work hard to model our lives after Jesus—a man who, during His ministry years, had no family, no home, and died at a fairly young age. Carl Jung once suggested that Western men in general become confused about life as they move past their 30s because Jesus, who died at 33, cannot provide a model for what later life looks like.

This is getting closer to the root of the issue. Christian men lack a foundational story that forms how they think about ways to integrate family and mission. I shared in this confusion as a son of the Western church until I encountered a Hebraic culture in Jerusalem where married men follow Abraham as a model for fatherhood. Observant Jewish fathers have a model that roots them to the home and the results are telling. Within orthodox Jewish families, more than 95% of kids identify with the faith of their parents. That means kids growing up in a committed Christian family are fifteen times more likely to lose their faith than kids growing up in committed Jewish households.

How should we as Christ-followers respond? Consider this radical thought: maybe Jesus never intended for his missionary lifestyle to become a model for married men raising families! Maybe Jesus believed His followers would be formed by both the Hebrew Scriptures and His teachings. The disciples certainly were. We know that both Peter and James would bring their wives with them on mission. Paul said some of the strongest statements about the importance of family and that to fail to provide for one's family was to deny the faith (1 Timothy 5:8).

Maybe Western Christians are suffering from a faith informed entirely by New Testament stories. We even call the Hebrew Scriptures "the Old Testament," which seems to imply they are far less relevant to us today.

So, fathers, maybe we need to add to our WWJD New Testament faith a new question: WWAD or What Would Abraham Do? Abraham had a radical and dangerous missionary calling as well and even though it meant leaving his father's house, he took his own household with him. I guess the Billy Graham Evangelistic Association thought it would have been too expensive, distracting, disruptive, and unstrategic to bring their families on mission with them as they traveled the world.

But consider this: who is leading the Billy Graham Evangelistic Association today? Franklin Graham, the same son who struggled to recognize his father during his childhood. What would have been more strategic for the long-term mission of the Billy Graham Evangelistic Association than for Franklin, their future leader, who nearly lost his faith in his early twenties, to have been with his father throughout his childhood?

Abraham left no family member behind, and neither should you.

I believe Billy Graham was a great man, and we as Christians are so fortunate for his life and legacy. But Western Christian fathers must learn to found their faith and practice on the entire Bible and remember that we are both followers of Jesus and sons of Abraham (Galatians 3:29).

09

NO ONE EVER TOLD ME I COULD BUILD AN ARMY

After participating in the Family Teams Weekend, we asked one dad in his early 40s what about the content stood out to him. His response was that, "no one ever told me before that I could build an army."

Now, we never explicitly said that fathers could or should build an army, but I love this takeaway because it illustrates one of the reasons I want this to get this multigenerational-team-on-mission paradigm out to as many young dads as possible.

The modern Western idea of family is almost entirely dominated by the aspects of family that are maternal. We think of the best families as those characterized by nurturing maternal love from both the mom and dad, and we imagine the family like a nest from which the children will one day fly far away and start lovely nests of their own.

Then we sit back and wonder why so many dads disconnect from their families at alarming rates. Why?

One reason: we've bought into the wrong family vision. The Bible does not present the idea of family that we have chosen in modern Western culture. This vision is basically devoid of mission or team or multigenerational continuity. Our maternal vision of family makes many men feel that the father is optional.

The biblical idea of family is quite different. In Genesis we learn that families were designed to be teams meant to rule together (Genesis 1:26-28).

Over in the New Testament, Paul writes in Ephesians that families are a place where fathers train children. When Paul had one thing to say to fathers, he didn't tell them to nurture children but to train them. Train them for what?

And now we come to one of the clearest passages in the Bible: Psalm 127, which tells us that children are a blessing, particularly for men in their youth, so that those children can be successful when they contend with the family enemies at the gate.

Did you know you are preparing your family for war? Do you know that you will need a well-trained army, because without one, those you love the most are likely to become casualties?

It's so dangerous to imagine your home only as a nest where children are to be sheltered from all danger for as long as possible. No, our homes are intended to be forward-operating outposts of the Kingdom of God, and there are enemies at the gate trying to breach the walls. Having well-trained kids actually matters in this battle, so we must let dads know that yes, you are building an army.

A family is a multigenerational team on mission; cultivating nothing more than a nurturing, nest-like environment is a strategic error. We don't live in peacetime. Dad, your army is being called up to go into battle to defend and expand the Kingdom of our Heavenly Father, and you have a finite amount of time to prepare.

Of course there are many other aspects to the family, and creating a nurturing environment is certainly important while kids are young and vulnerable, but to limit the family to that vision is a strategic error that will cost the family dearly.

Remember the words of Charles Baudelaire: "The greatest trick the Devil ever pulled was convincing the world he didn't exist." Dads, don't fall for this trick.

As you establish a home of love, peace, and Gospel-inspired forgiveness keep in mind that your family team has a purpose: to pierce into the Kingdom of darkness and not be overcome by the forces arrayed against it. And remember the key to winning this war: God's chosen man for that job is you. You can do this. You have the Holy Spirit, the Scriptures, your wife and the Church to support you. Build and train your army, and may your family be successful when they contend with the enemies at the gate.

10

PURSUING THE HEART OF YOUR MOST DISCONNECT-ED CHILD

Many of my friends are having a larger number of kids compared to the average Western family. We have been inspired by the high calling and gift of getting to be fathers, as well as the meaning in building multigenerational family teams. But as the number of members on the team grows, dads of larger families need to pay close attention to one specific thing: what is going on in the heart of your most disconnected child.

When it seems all your kids are thriving except one, there is a temptation to subtly blame or discount the feelings of that one struggling child. Be careful here. Inside of his or her heart often lurks the lesson you most need to learn, and the one you're most reluctant to face.

There's a scene in the landmark film *The Neverending Story* where the hero Atreyu must pass "The Magic Mirror Gate." Atreyu will have to look his true self in the face. His friend brushes off this challenge saying, "So? That shouldn't be so hard." But the wise man in the story retorts, "Oh, that's what everyone thinks! But kind people find out that they are cruel. Brave men find out that they are really cowards! Confronted by their true selves, most men run away, screaming!"

Facing the problems in the heart of your most disconnected child is like looking into The Magic Mirror Gate, and that's why so many of us dads would rather avoid dealing with what's going on with that child: because it forces us to deal with hidden parts of our own hearts.

There's a practical reason why this child often points out deep weakness or inadequacy. Consider basic team dynamics. Imagine any team that has five diverse members and a strong leader or coach. Typically the style of that coach will really resonate with some of the members more than others. Those team members will begin to really thrive while others will continue to struggle. But it's inevitable that one will struggle the most. Maybe there's something about the coach's approach that just doesn't resonate or reach that team member. At first this team member isn't sure how to think about this disconnect, especially if they see others enjoying the coach's leadership.

Now imagine that there's nothing you can do to ever get off this team. Year after year, this team consumes a huge percentage of your time, and your place on this team is a huge part of your identity. What happens to you if the coach never succeeds at creating a strong connection? You may take on a new identity and begin to see yourself as the anti-team member, the one who doesn't fit or belong, the proverbial black sheep of the family.

But let's back up. Long before this occurs, there's something every dad can do to prevent their kids from adopting the black sheep identity. Choose now to regularly identify which one of your kids you feel most disconnected from, and then do whatever it takes to understand what is going on in his or her heart. Which child is most disconnected can change from time to time, so it's important to keep identifying your most disconnected child.

God has gifted you with a diverse set of team members, and one of them needs something that you struggle to provide. What's likely happening is this child's greatest need is matching up with one of your weaknesses. They likely can't articulate that exact weakness, but they will show you through their feelings and actions.

First, it's important to accept full responsibility for the weak areas in your own leadership. Sure, the child is going to have flaws that contribute to the disconnection, and when you're fully connected with your child relationally, you can address those issues, but make it your first instinct to focus on your own areas of weakness.

Then it's time to define the problem. You need to be crystal clear in labelling the issue so you can address it. The more time you spend understanding what is going on in the heart of your struggling child, the more you'll begin to identify how your own leadership style may have contributed to the issue. Then, make an action plan. This might include learning about this area, but it's most important that you begin to overcome this weakness through a concrete change in behavior.

Here are three examples of my own leadership weaknesses that have hurt my kids:

1. **Discomfort with direct commands.** I don't like people directly telling me what to do; consequently I don't like directly telling other people what to do. I prefer making vague suggestions. I've had to embrace the process of bringing my kids together and directly spelling out what I

want done.

2. **Lack of one-on-one time.** I enjoy being alone and I don't like awkward silence, so I wouldn't initiate enough one-on-one time with my kids. I've now made a discipline of doing this at least two times per week.

3. **Fear of spiritual intimacy.** I'm worried my kids are drifting spiritually and sometimes that worry results in not finding out the truth of how they are doing. I've had to make it a discipline to ask.

Personally, I feel like I'm just beginning to learn how to be a leader. I have so much farther to go but I believe that if we stay close to the hearts of every single one of our kids and refuse to give up on any of them, they will teach us how to become better leaders and will grow to love us and bond with us through the process.

11

MY FIRST WORK DAY WITH MY DAUGHTER

Fifteen years ago I sat in a Board of Directors meeting with a man investing in our first company, and in the room as well were his three sons. Sometime during the middle of that three-hour meeting I suddenly realized that this man gets to spend more time with his sons now in their 30s than most fathers spend with their kids when they are young and living in the house.

I had never even considered this before. I had only seen children grow up get a job and move away from their parents with the hope they could be reunited over Christmas or Thanksgiving.

And even while the kids are in the house most dads spend the majority of their time at work away from their families, so there's a depth of relationship they may never achieve with their children unless they find some way to integrate their kids into their work lives.

So I made a specific decision at that moment. My oldest daughter was three at the time, and I decided to steer my work life in such a way that if any of my kids wanted to work with me when they entered the workforce, then that would at least be an option open to them. It's not a demand or even an expectation; I just wanted it to be an option.

Now I know that even voicing this desire sets off alarm bells for some of you. Our culture is obsessed with the horror story of parents being too narrow in their vision for their children. Movies from *The Little Mermaid* to *Horton Hears a Who* tell us and our kids that nothing is more dangerous than a parent having a specific vision for their children. Virtually every animated blockbuster is based on this trope film critic Stephen Greydanus calls "Junior Knows Best". This stems from a sacred doctrine of modern Western culture that the individual is not finding their destiny unless it's unencumbered by any direction or even influence from the past generation.

While there are certainly ways to smother your kids through manipulating them to follow your self-centered vision, it's important to remember that there's a danger on the other side as well. We believe in forcing our kids to "find themselves" while, at the same time, slamming the door on even the possibility that they might find part of their path in and through the family. But why not make it an option? Why not leave that door open? Why not pursue big things as a family and invite your kids to consider serving those initiatives, whether it be businesses, ministries, projects, or causes where their unique talents, gifts, and callings can be released in efforts organized and led by and through your family?

Last week I sat in my office in a familiar weekday morning meeting—and my daughter was in the room, fully engaged in her new job working for our organization. The meeting content was nothing special—just normal, mundane projects to be organized and managed—but everything about that meeting was filled with special meaning for me because I was getting to do these things in partnership with my daughter. I'm sure this experience will come and go. I'm sure she'll spend years serving her husband, kids, and other organizations, or need to travel to places far from our home, but having open doors into my work if and when it makes sense for her and my other kids has been a worthwhile effort. Because doing my normal work in those moment means more than just getting work done—it means directly investing in the relationships that will build our multi-generational family.

12

WISDOM IS LIVING TO BLESS YOUR GRANDCHIL-DREN

How often do men in their 20s think about their future grandchildren? Maybe in some college dorm somewhere in the world you'll find a group of guys discussing in excited tones, late into the night, their dreams to bless their future grandchildren, but if such a conversation is happening, it's probably very rare and probably not in the West. And this is unfortunate, because to aim your life at the flourishing of your family line at the earliest age possible is to be on the path both to changing the world and to living a great life.

Wisdom has entered the heart of a young man who chooses to aim his life in a direction that will bless his future grandchildren. Decisions like: finding a wife who will bring fruitfulness and stability to his household; choosing a career that will allow him the time to be with his kids; and making financial investments that pay dividends far beyond his short lifespan. Proverbs 13:22 says, "A good man leaves an inheritance to his children's children." Being this proverbial "good man" is not simply about money; it's about all the tiny day-to-day decisions you make differently when you're aiming for a goal far into the future.

You may wonder, why not say instead, "Wisdom is living to bless your children"? Why talk about the unique wisdom inherent in living for one's grandchildren? Because living with only two generations in view, your generation and your child's generation, gives rise to subtle decisions that often inadvertently result in building a terminal generation, particularly when it comes to parenting your kids. *I'm not training my kids to live a great individual life, I'm training my kids to be great parents.* This perspective has given me the will to be more intentional with my kids, knowing that problematic relational or behavior patterns are not just something that maybe I should just learn to put up with but problems that will impact my future grandchildren—and I have a limited number of years to coach my kids through these issues.

Let me give you just one really practical example. If you want to see what issues in microcosm your kids will have in parenting one day, give them a pet and make them exclusively responsible for that pet's care. Now I know this can be a nightmare for many parents, because their child will drop the ball repeatedly and the parent knows the pet will suffer unless we step in to pick up the slack. So little Johnny's pet quickly becomes our responsibility. But what I can't stop thinking about in those moments is how my grandchildren will pay the price if I don't help my child work through whatever selfish, neglectful, absent-minded, overbearing patterns are already emerging within their still-forming character. When's a better time to work on these issues then when they're under your training?

Moving from the practical day-to-day to the spiritual, consider what David said about God's commitment to David's grandchildren and to the grandchildren of all those who fear him. David wrote in Psalm 103:17, "the steadfast love of the Lord is from everlasting to everlasting on those who fear him, and his righteousness to their children's children". Did you know it is possible for you to accumulate spiritual blessings during your lifetime that will someday be enjoyed by your grandchildren? God stated this on Mount Sinai in Exodus 34 when He showed Moses His glory and declared, "I am slow to anger and filled with unfailing love and faithfulness. I lavish unfailing love to a thousand generations." Cultivating a deep relationship with your Heavenly Father is the most strategic thing you can do for both your life and your descendants.

And remember, there is no tension between blessing your grandchildren and blessing the rest of the world, because the more spiritually alive, well-trained grandchildren come from your family line, the more the force of your life will extend into the distant future as your family expands and multiplies through your descendants to bless the world that is to come.

13

BEWARE OF WISDOM YOU DIDN'T EARN

One of the most persistent misunderstandings modern Western culture makes is to equate intelligence, education and knowledge with wisdom. Perhaps there's no better illustration of this fact than to see the folly on display at some of the top University campuses in our country. These places are pillars of education and teeming with highly intelligent people who are shockingly devoid of wisdom.

I think JRR Tolkien illustrated the surprising difference between intelligence and wisdom elegantly in *The Lord of the Rings* through the character of Samwise Gamgee. Sam is clearly less intelligent than most of his companions, but he embodies the wisdom of the diligent man and delivers piercing insights at the most unexpected times.

So what is wisdom and how can we get more of it? It's easy to get more knowledge in a world where Wikipedia and educational institutions abound, but wisdom remains strangely elusive. One of my favorite definitions of wisdom is "skill with regard to the basic way the world works." The wise man has discovered basic patterns in life, in nature, and in relationships and can apply those insights to increasingly complex situations in a way that allows him to handle life with skill and apparent ease.

And that's why I was struck by this quote by Carl Jung: "Beware of wisdom you didn't earn." I've been pondering this statement for months, and it seems to expose one of the more dangerous tendencies men have in general, as well as one I've seen in my own life. We want the shortcut, the quick path, the easy way. Back in the Garden, our work was cursed and ever since, we've been trying to find a way to escape toil, to avoid danger, to abdicate responsibility. We need wisdom but we don't want to earn it; we'd rather just know it. But wisdom doesn't quite work like that. Wisdom is a skill, and skills must be honed by practice, discipline, and perseverance.

Bringing this down into our daily lives: are you overwhelmed by all of your responsibilities? Are things hard at work and frustrating at home? Do you wonder if it's worth it? Are you tempted to give up? If you are in these circumstances and are asking God "Why?" one perspective to keep in mind is that maybe you are slowly, steadily earning wisdom.

Your soul is being shaped to rule and you're taking Wisdom 101 (or maybe 401). So please don't quit. Don't lose heart. And don't think something ultimately tragic has befallen you. Yes, there are real tragedies in a fallen world, but more often our hard days are more like toiling on a treasure hunt.

Solomon, the wisest man who ever lived said wisdom is more precious than jewels. Like jewels, wisdom is created by bearing up under the grinding weight of years. This is God's gift to us as fathers, putting weight on our backs beyond our current capacity to endure in order to build up in us the strength of wisdom.

And, by the way, we must, in turn, let our own children struggle under heavy burdens. Because few things are more dangerous to society than to send young adults out into the world, puffed up with knowledge and in possession of unearned wisdom. There is no easy button in the process of attaining wisdom. Our Father has made the world well and if we let our Father's world shape us, we'll discover the jewels of soul wisdom preparing us to reign in His coming Kingdom.

14

REBUKING PARENTS

If you're the parent of a child under the age of twenty, you're likely part of the first generation of parents where most of us have taken several psychology classes, read a handful of self-help books, and maybe even spent some time in private counseling, and one inescapable conclusion you've likely reached is that your parents screwed you up. This conclusion is almost certainly true. Every year psychology unearths more and deeper ways we are impacted by our upbringing, and specifically by our parents.

The more you think about all the ways your parents failed you or hurt you, it can become more and more difficult to resist growing bitter. The clearest definition of bitterness I've ever heard is, "The decision to hold onto hurt when we feel someone has taken something from us that we are powerless to get back in the hope that we can get justice for what we've lost."

When you feel your parents did something unjust to you, you tend to spend the rest of your life feeling they owe you such an enormous debt that even small irritations can trigger deep emotions. This can wreak havoc on any attempt to enfold the older generation into a multigenerational vision.

Now there are certainly different degrees of damage parents can do to their children, and while some situations represent a clear and present threat to your current children, others are more the product of past hurts and sins that are an unfortunate part of family life in a fallen world. And into that context Paul writes a surprising command to Timothy as a younger leader in the Church at Ephesus: "Do not rebuke an older man but encourage him as you would a father" (1 Timothy 5:1).

Note how Paul phrased this instruction. He seems to be saying, "We both know that you would never rebuke your own father, so be sure to treat older men in the church the same way you would your father." But we don't live in a culture where we have set rules of honor and respect that are well-known and practiced by a younger generation to their parents' generation. What would it look like to take this command seriously in our day?

Paul is clearly saying that kids are never to rebuke parents. We're free from the obligation to try to exact justice or even the need to harshly correct parents in areas they've wronged us. That doesn't mean we shouldn't have open and honest conversations with our parents, but rather that we must make sure our comments in those conversations don't cross the line and become a rebuke. And I don't think that's because parents never deserve a rebuke! Just about everyone deserves a rebuke. It's just that a rebuke, according to Paul, shouldn't come from a parent's children. We probably know the areas where our parents need to be rebuked better than anyone, yet Paul is indicating we're supposed to limit ourselves to only encouraging our parents.

Why? Why not take your list of grievances and let your parents know all the ways they've failed you and messed you up? One likely reason is to protect the environment needed to maintain healthy relationships across the generations. But all rebukes are risky and could be relationally damaging; Paul tells Timothy in his next letter that there is a time to rebuke those in the church (2 Timothy 3:16). Why not parents?

Paul spells out the reason a few verses later when he gives instruction about widows: "If a widow has children or grandchildren, these should learn first of all to put their religion into practice by caring for their own family and so repaying their parents and grandparents, for this is pleasing to God" (1 Timothy 5:4). In other words, your parents don't owe you, you owe your parents and even your grandparents a debt you can never repay. When you owe someone an unpayable debt and then rebuke them like they owe you, your actions do not honor the true story. Your feeling of righteous indignation for all the ways your parents harmed you may be downplaying the other side of the story. This story includes all the ways your parents cared for you and provided for you for all the years you were completely helpless. If your parents made those sacrifices, then you have accumulated, in God's eyes, a debt of honor you owe them.

As I write this, my parents moved into our home earlier this week, and I feel so blessed to be able to give to them without reservation in the final season of their lives because I'm not given the assignment to fix them. I'm given the obligation to honor them, to care for them, and to, as this verse says, "encourage them".

Parent-rebuking is becoming so common in this generation that it almost feels like a new pastime. In a culture that feels like everything we receive is simply an entitlement and where there's no end to what we feel we are owed.

We must find ways to work through the bitterness many of us are carrying toward our parents so we can protect and build our multigenerational families. And let's please keep in mind: we're all in the process of screwing up our own children and we all hope one day our kids will forgive and then encourage us. Let's be careful not to destroy the ground of grace upon which each of us will spend our final decades standing.

15

RECEIVING GOD AS OUR MODEL FATHER

Why did God choose to reveal himself as a father?

When Jesus first taught His disciples to pray He told them to begin by saying the surprising words, "Our Father".

Paul instructs believers that one of Holy Spirit's main ministries is to help our hearts say to God, "Abba, Father."

When we're born we don't yet fully understand the concept of father. It's like an empty bucket that our earthly fathers spend the next twenty years filling through their actions and inactions. Every one of us has strong emotional triggers to what our fathers placed in that bucket; those formative experiences determine our visceral reaction to the concept we call fatherhood.

Then God comes and says, "you know that thing called a father? That's what I'm like and that's who I am. I'd like to be your Father." Then each of us looks inside our bucket and wonders whether we want to have a relationship with God if he's like what we find in there.

Paul Vitz, Professor of Psychology at the University of New York, made an interesting discovery when he peered into the personal lives of famous atheists and famous Christians. He detailed his findings in a book called *Faith of the Fatherless: The Psychology of Atheism*. Here's a summary: "By studying the lives of numerous famous militant atheists, from the old atheists Nietzsche, Sartre, and Freud to the new atheists..., Vitz discovers a startling common pattern: atheism arises in people with dead, absent, or abusive fathers. By contrast, prominent defenders of religious belief— including Blaise Pascal, William Wilberforce, and G.K. Chesterton— were blessed with attentive, loving, and caring fathers."

God made quite a risky decision to reveal himself as a father. Or to say that more accurately, God is a Father, and He decided to give us earthly fathers so we'd have an idea of what He is like.

That's why we all need to think deeply about what's in our bucket called fatherhood.

We need to take out that bucket, dump out its contents, and really sort out which actions, characteristics and elements reflect God's Fatherhood and which do not.

We begin our lives looking to our fathers to understand God, but when we mature, we look to God to understand fatherhood.

This is the critical transition.

When we're young, we have no choice but to understand fatherhood primarily through our earthly fathers. But something changes as we grow up. The older we get, the more we must allow our growing knowledge of God and his nature to refine our vision of fatherhood.

The author of Hebrews makes this comparison in chapter 12 when he writes, "Since we respected our earthly fathers who disciplined us, shouldn't we submit even more to the discipline of the Father of our spirits, and live forever?"

What does this mean practically? Three things:

1. Guard carefully what remains in your own bucket called fatherhood. If your earthly father did things that were ungodly, you need to clean those items out of concept of fatherhood. That wasn't them being a father; that was an expression of their fallen humanity.
2. Be careful what you put into your kids' fatherhood buckets. We will all make many mistakes, but we have a lot of control over whether our kids will love or hate the idea of fatherhood. We get to shape their initial reactions to the concept of fatherhood and that is a great responsibility.
3. Let God's character continually inform and reform your understand of what it means to be a father.

Our earthly fathers are our surrogates for understanding fatherhood. We needed them to get started on this journey of understanding the nature of a father, but we must intentionally exchange their imperfect modeling for God's perfect modelling of fatherhood. We must allow God, our Abba Father, to show us the true heart of the father. By doing this we'll both deepen our intimacy with God and grow to become better reflections of God's character to our own children.

16

WANT TO BUILD YOUR FAMILY? LAY DOWN YOUR LIFE FOR YOUR WIFE

Sometimes when men get a hold of a vision to build their family into a multigenerational team on mission, they click into hyper-productivity mode. They start to think about having more kids, about hosting more people, about engaging their parents, maybe even their siblings, about improving their house, about owning assets, about having more home-cooked meals. And as the vision grows and the tasks and projects multiply, there's another person who, at the same time, is watching her life get harder, more busy, and more complex, only she often has less power to slow down the rate of change. Even more tasks may be piling onto her plate and she may not have received the same sudden burst of team building excitement. And that person, of course, is your wife.

So what do you when you're wanting to run after this vision at 100mph and your wife is starting to reach for the brakes? Should you just keep going and insist she keep up? Shouldn't she simply match your energy and level of interest? After all, isn't she supposed to help you? I've noticed a pattern in some men, myself included: when we get a new passion for our family that didn't exist last week, we often expect our wives to magically have a similar surge of energy. But it rarely works like that. She is a human being, just like you, with her own interests, her own struggles with energy. She's going through her own seasons, wrestling with her own hopes and doubts. So what's a husband and father to do when he finds himself out of sync in some way with his wife when wanting to expand or improve their family?

Let me ask this question in a slightly different way: when you develop a huge passion for building your family, where do you channel that energy first? The intuitive place to focus that energy is onto your kids or your family culture, and then maybe onto your extended family. And if that's the order of the way you think you build a family, you're entering the danger zone. The Bible actually answers the question of what to do when you want to build a family, but it sounds counterintuitive at first. The Bible doesn't say to lay down your life for your family; it says to lay down your life for your wife.

"Husbands," Paul writes, "love your wives as Christ loved the church and gave himself up for her." (Ephesians 5). Why did he say that? Why didn't he say, "love your *family* as Christ loved the church"? There is a divine order to family-building and it starts with and is sustained by the ongoing sacrificial love of the husband toward his wife.

A family is built on the foundation of that kind of active love. She is not an accessory to your family. She is not on the lowest rung on the family pyramid. God gives the husband authority over the home and intends the husband to use that authority to lay down his life for his wife. That is what Christ did with His authority. It's this giving of sacrificial love that results in the fruit of a beautiful family. Strong families are, at their core, the byproduct of men lovingly laying down their lives for their wives.

So if you want to build a family, start by laying down your life for your wife.

17

TODAY SALVATION HAS COME TO THIS HOUSE

Growing up in the evangelical movement, a movement whose theology emerged almost entirely in America, none of us would probably be surprised if we were to discover that a large dose of hyper-individualism may have smuggled its way into our doctrines.

One sacred belief that at least deserves a second look in light of a multigenerational mindset is that salvation is a 100% individual affair. "Your family has absolutely no impact on your salvation" I was taught. "God has only children, He has no grandchildren", was the famous phrase that stuck in my head, along with, "Salvation is a deeply personal choice between you and God alone," as we closed our eyes, bowed our heads and often raised our hands to receive salvation individually while no one was looking.

While I continue to believe this idea in principle, it seems to mask or at least miss a theme repeatedly described in the New Testament. That theme is the phenomenon of household salvation. Why is this talked about so often in the Bible, yet I've never once seen or heard anyone talk about this phenomenon in my lifetime as an American Christian? It's left me concerned that maybe we're missing something. So instead of resolving this question, since I don't have a great answer, I'm just going to explore it and let us wrestle with the tension for a minute.

Let's start with Jesus. We've probably all heard the story of this short tax collector named Zacchaeus and his encounter with Jesus while up a sycamore tree. What we might remember less easily was the statement Jesus made after Zacchaeus repented. Jesus declared, "Today salvation has come to this house." Huh, why this house? Was this just an ancient way of saying Zacchaeus as an individual was saved? But then again maybe more was saved than just Zach as an individual?

Next let's turn to Acts, where the vast majority of the salvations in the New Testament are recorded. What do we find there?

The first Gentile salvation to be recorded was a Roman centurion named Cornelius when an angel appears to him and says, "Send to Joppa for Simon who is called Peter. He will bring you a message through which you and all your household will be saved" (Acts 11:13-14). What strikes me here is Cornelius as an individual is told he will be saved, while separately he is also told his household will be saved as well. Even though we learn from the story that God was sending Peter to share the Gospel with Cornelius because of what he as an individual did for the poor, the blessing spilled over and in some way included his entire household.

Moving on to Acts 16, you have Paul and Silas in prison in Philippi, and when the jailer asks what he can do to be saved, Paul gives this curious response: "Believe in the Lord Jesus, and you will be saved—you and your household." Again two salvations—the individual and the household.

We also hear of a household salvation occurring in Acts 18 when we read, "Crispus, the synagogue leader, and his entire household believed in the Lord." It seems clear in these instances that the individual household members are also believing, but at the same time there's a clear connection between the faith of the household leader and the faith of the individual household members.

What exactly is this connection, and was this only true in the first century? Maybe this no longer has any application today in the Western world? I thought that might be the case, but then I read a study done by the Swiss government of faith in their country as part of their census in the year 2000. This study discovered, "if a father does not go to church, no matter how faithful his wife's devotion, only one child in 50 will become a regular worshipper. If a father goes regularly, regardless of the practice of the mother, between two-thirds and three-quarters of their children will become churchgoers." Keep in mind this was just an accidental discovery based on their national census data.

Clearly there's an under-explored, underrated, under-reported connection here between the faith of the leader of the household and the faith of his entire household. So whatever that means theologically, I'd like to say to the fathers out there: do not underestimate the impact your spiritual life is having on your family generationally.

Way back in Genesis 12, God calls Abraham and tells him that through his family, "all the families of the world will be blessed." This is the place in Scripture where God begins to outline the details of His salvation plan; He says that this salvation will happen through Abraham's family in order to bless the families of the world. Maybe God's plan for salvation is more family-centered than we think. Maybe the day you came to faith it could be said to you, "Today salvation has come to this house."

18

THE FATHERHOOD SCHOOL OF FINANCE

Back in 2000, my family was virtually penniless but happily serving the Lord. We got by week-to-week by the grace of God (and the generosity of churchgoers). I didn't think of money as a problem. In fact, it's safe to say I didn't think about money at all. April was skilled at stretching every dollar that came in while I stayed entirely focused on ministry. And that's when it happened. The church insisted I spend years focusing on a project outside of my calling. Instead of doing a half-hearted job, I felt the right thing was to resign, but I literally could not afford to say no. I felt trapped and it made me miserable. I felt I could only continue to provide for my family at the cost of my integrity. After a couple of weeks wrestling through our response I decided to resign and cry out to the Lord to rescue me and my family.

He did, but not in the way I expected (a new job) or the way I wanted (a pile of cash). He sent me a mentor to teach me about finances. His name was Robert Kiyosaki.

I ran across his book called *Rich Dad, Poor Dad,* read it, and then spent the next year reading every book he had written or recommended until his view of finances became a basic part of the way I thought about money.

Today my family still has many problems, but one of them is not a lack of financial resources. I believe most people's financial problems are not in their bank account but in their heads and in their hearts. If you struggle with finances, please invest in your financial education.

Being financially educated is not only about making money because in a modern economy, financial literacy is necessary even when simply attempting save money for future generations. Why? Because there's an unseen robber of your future family's assets.

If your daughter burst into your room and said, "Dad, there's a thief in our house!" you would do your best to protect your family. What you need to know is there is a thief in your house and he has moved in permanently. But what's even worse is that you and I do not have the power to get rid of him. All we can do is constantly stand between this thief and our family's assets and attempt to counter him blow by blow, in a constant duel to protect your family's future. This is our job because we are fathers.

Who is this thief? Let me illustrate. If you lived in the year 1800 and buried $1000 in the backyard of your family home and your great-great-grandchildren dug it up one hundred years later in 1900, it would have roughly the same purchasing power. If it could buy a hundred rifles in 1800, it would still buy a hundred rifles in 1900. But if you buried that $1000 in 1900 and dug it up in the year 2000, it would be worth about 90% less. For your family, that's the same as if someone came and stole $900 of the $1000. And they didn't even have to know where you buried it! And it's not as if that $900 disappeared. Someone actually took it, spent it, and enjoyed it at you and your family's expense. So what can we as fathers do about it?

This is what happens to cash when a country or bank has the power to print money and devalue their currency. You can't just work harder and stash away cash for decades for your grandchildren. The world is not that simple anymore. I wish it was! Money is no longer tied to anything fixed, which may violate a form of justice described in Proverbs 20:10: "False weights and unequal measures—the Lord detests double standards of every kind." But this is the world you and your family live in, and as fathers we need to learn about it and work to protect our families.

Yes, there are things that should be done at the political level, but this is unlikely to change in the near future and so, in the meantime, this means you must go to the Fatherhood School of Financial Literacy if you hope to provide for your family's future. The middle class will likely begin to melt away in the face of this resource drain, and you and I must step up to fulfill the mandate Scripture gives to families to stay financially stable so we can have enough resources to bless others (1 Thessalonians 4:11-12).

Practically, what does this mean? When we choose to try to build a multigenerational family inside of an economy of endless inflation we must consider strategies like:

- Wisely investing and saving
- Acquiring and managing cash-flowing assets
- Training our children at a young age to understand economics
- Planning to provide for our parents if/when they lose their retirement
- Considering becoming an expert in at least one way of

making money in an area of the economy that is increasing in value

We can't abdicate this responsibility or simply choose to entrust our family's long-term security to others. We need to build strong, financially stable families now more than ever. This is one way we learn to become sons of our Father and prepare for the day when we'll be ministers in His future government.

19

HOW TO BLESS YOUR CHILDREN AFTER YOU DIE

God only knows how many days each of us has left. When we're gone, our children and their children will live on and, no matter what we do, the plain truth is, we won't be there to help them. This is a scary thought for any father who loves his family.

And so I was deeply struck by a statement made in an interview by Randy Pausch, the famous terminally ill professor who gave "The Last Lecture". When Randy was asked about his family, he perfectly expressed the true heart of a father facing his own mortality,

"The metaphor I've used is... somebody's going to push my family off a cliff pretty soon, and I won't be there to catch them. And that breaks my heart. But I have some time to sew some nets to cushion the fall. So, I can curl up in a ball and cry, or I can get to work on the nets."

But how do you sew these nets? What are they made of? And should we wait to break out the needle and thread until we have been given a death sentence, since we all know death is coming for each of likely at a time we don't expect?

Where can we find that perfect life insurance policy that is guaranteed to take care of our family? There is only one way you can be sure your family will be protected and blessed after you die: you have to receive a promise from an undying Being of absolute power who keeps His word forever. If such a thing exists it should be the top priority of every wise father to do anything he can, to invest whatever it costs, to secure that promise.

One of the first narratives in all of Scripture describes how one father received such a promise. God gave to Abraham a promise of blessing that he could pass on to his children and his children's children throughout all the generations his family continued on the earth (Genesis 12:1-3, Genesis 15 & 17). And if you study how Abraham captured God's heart, you learn that it was through a lifelong practice of reckless faith (Hebrews 11:8-12), of act after act that would appear to outsiders as irresponsible for a loving father. His unquestioning trust in God and the beautiful friendship they built brought these covenant promises into his family, and they are still active and impacting his family to this day.

But what about us? Are there any modern-day examples of family blessings?

On January 8, 1956 Nate Saint, along with four friends, were killed in an act of reckless faith, trying to bring the Gospel to the violent Waodani people during Operation Auca, deep within the rainforest of Ecuador. Many people would look at that decision as disastrous because these five men left young families with no one to protect them—no nets—but anyone who thinks this way does not know the heart of God who is "the helper of the fatherless" (Psalm 10:14).

Skip forward 56 years and Nate Saint's son Steve, who has dedicated his life to aviation in missions work, just like his father, does something that billions of dollars in the aviation industry and billions of dollars in the automotive industry have been unable to do: Steve Saint invented the first viable, FAA certified, flying car.

Jesus said in Mark 8:35, "For whoever wants to save their life will lose it, but whoever loses their life for me and for the gospel will save it." And I'd add: if you want God to bless your family, if you want nets that will last, then offer up your entire life in reckless faith, in total trust, and God will not only build nets for your family, but also engines to propel your family forward. So if you die a little bit earlier, your family will still be more safe under God's protection than under yours.

For the Scriptures declare that God is "A father to the fatherless, a defender of widows" (Psalm 68:5). And if death does come we know that "Precious in the sight of the LORD is the death of his saints" (Psalm 116:15).

20

CONTROLLING CHAOS VS. OBEDIENCE TRAINING

I love training my children. There are few things more exhilarating than watching a self-centered, flesh-dominated, God-hating, sin-loving little rebel steadily transform into a soft-hearted, God-loving, others-serving contributing member of the family.

But I've noticed lately that my passion is not shared by many around me. This confused me for a long time, but I think I'm just now beginning to see possibly why. Most parents actually don't *train* their children—and Christian parents seem to be no exception—but almost all parents still *discipline* their children. When I would see a parent discipline their child, I assumed it was for the purpose of training, but as I've observed more families over time, I've discovered their discipline is not really training but is for the purpose of controlling chaos. The two are quite different.

Here's an example: You're at a public place with your kids and a couple of friends and their kids, and you begin to realize your child is being too rowdy, loud, and disruptive. You call to your son Johnny as he walks by, saying, "Johnny, come here, I want to talk to you." But he's having too much fun so he ignores you, pretending to not hear. "Johnny," you call more loudly this time. He ignores you again. Now you're realizing you're causing as much noise as he ever did and he's quieting down so you go back to your conversation.

I've seen this scenario so many times and it has often puzzled me. My thought hasn't been judging the parent but more curious as to why they were willing to let that perfect training opportunity pass them by. I value the moments when my children deliberately defy me or my wife because they provide a clear opportunity to reinforce the child's need to obey his or her parents (Ephesians 6:1).

But in the above scenario, I've watched parents ignore sometimes ten opportunities in a thirty-minute conversation. What is going on here? This is my hypothesis. These parents aren't trying to train their children to obey—they are trying to control chaos. Their discipline is based on the amount of chaos they can handle at a given time. Deliberate disobedience is far less of a concern, therefore, instead of learning to monitor their own behavior, the child learns to monitor their parent's mood and the situation closely, discerning the things they can get away with.

This is a disaster for kids. It makes the parents' patience and tolerance the real trigger for discipline instead of the child's behavior and trains kids how to manipulate a situation rather than how to obey. This leads the child to routinely push his or her parents to the edge since they have been systematically trained to find that edge of tolerance and keep their parents there continuously. How exhausting for the parents! How unfortunate for the children. And when these parents see an obedient child, their reaction is, "I wish my child had that temperament". So they blame their child when they have spent years training their children to behave in this manner.

There's a better, easier way and it starts when a parent chooses to learn and embrace obedience training.

The next question you may be asking is, "How do I train my kids? Nothing works!" I used to think the lack of equipping around training was the root of the problem until I started to observe these same parents when they were potty training their kids or when their kids had a peanut allergy. Magically the parents transformed into amazing trainers educating their kids, rewarding their kids and correcting their kids in creative and effective ways. They asked others for help, read books, googled their questions, and kept at it until their child was well-trained.

In other words, the problem is not that we don't know how to train our kids to obey, it's that we don't believe in it.

Be honest: when you correct your kids, is it because of a desire to train them or because they have finally crossed a line that wore out your patience? If it's the latter, then you likely believe parenting is more about controlling chaos than training. And to that I'd ask you dads to reconsider this verse, the only command directly given to fathers in the entire New Testament: "Fathers, do not exasperate your children; instead, bring them up in the training and instruction of the Lord (Ephesians 6:4)."

21

AN ODE TO MY DAD

by April Pryor

A few years back, several families in our community started teaching their kids to call their dads "Papa." If I remember correctly, this was in response to the "sonship" concept and wanting to help our children deepen their identity as a child of God.

So I just observed it and felt no conviction to do the same. I understood what they were doing and that was cool; it just didn't transfer over to me. As I've thought of this off and on, I always thought, "Well, I would just start to teach my kids to call God 'Dad,' the name they already call their earthly father." But, since I don't do that myself, it never really went much further than that.

Anytime I started to think about it, I began to realize it was striking a chord of some kind and I would force myself to stop thinking about it. Like, it was too intimate to think about... don't go there. You see, I have a *very* special place in my heart for the word "Dad." It's reserved for Don Seely and *no other!* As a teenager and young woman, that place in my heart was held dear and no man was going to come near it.

When I got married, I "inherited" an amazing father-in-law, but he's just that, the father to my husband, not my "Dad." As a new bride, anytime I became confused between the role my husband and father played, my father would often win out in my heart. God, to me, is Father, Spirit, Son, Jesus, Savior, Creator, Lord—I can even try to think of Him as Lover and Groom—but *not* Dad.

I have slowly realized that this is a place in my heart—a very intimate, precious place—that I have withheld from God. Why? Because it just never occurred to me? At first, perhaps. Because He doesn't deserve it? Yes, I think that's why.

In my recent spiritual life, I have been begging for more of the Spirit. I see all over the early church in Scripture that people were speaking in tongues, getting saved, getting baptized with water, then getting baptized with the Spirit. Although the concept of the Spirit is relatively new to me, I still feel like I haven't experienced what I read in Scripture. I don't feel lonely; I know He's right by my side and has a plan for me and responds to me and loves me and is even pleased with me (as I've heard from others speaking words over me.) But I started to want more. *More,* Lord! More Spirit, please! I want more Spirit! I told Him I don't care how or what it looks like— I refuse to put Him in a box. I trust Him and will leave it up to Him to show Himself to me in a way special to us. I can't rely on myself to get through this life, to face my days that are full of me.

One day, as I was in a place of quiet with Him, I turned my iPod onto shuffle on my worship playlist and on came this song... one of those kind of annoying 14-minute-long Spirit-led worship times caught on tape that you can only listen to when you're in the right mood. The man was singing "I'm like a baby, like a baby, saying 'dada, dada, dada'. Help me Lord, I'm saying 'da—-da, da——da' Daddy, Daddy, Daddy! The Language of heaven." As I listened, something in me broke. I started crying like a baby, allowed the words to wash over me, opened my mouth, and started singing along with this man. At first it was really hard, even just to say "dada," but soon I was singing it out at the top of my lungs! "Dad!!!! Dad!!!! Dad!!!! Dad!!!!!" Thank you. Thank you. Thank you. This was a very profound experience and I found it too intimate to even speak about with anyone. I meditated on it for a few days. I couldn't even journal about it.

A few weeks later, at our Story-Formed-Life Bible Study, we were discussing Galatians 3:6: "And because we are his children, God has sent the Spirit of his Son into our hearts, prompting us to call out, 'Abba, Father.'" Whoa! It hit me like a ton of bricks! There was the Spirit I had been begging for! I held on to His arm long enough to allow His Spirit to penetrate me to prompt me to call out "Dad! Dad! Dad!" So does He deserve that title? Yes, because He adopted me.

What a tribute to my earthly dad. Thanks, Don Seely, for making and being such a special place in my heart, that, once I discovered it, boosted me into a new level of faith with my first Dad. You have stewarded me well.

The other night, I was having a very sweet heart-to-heart with my only son, where he was sharing with me some of his deep struggles. We concluded that we needed to take these issues to the Lord and without taking a breath, he broke into prayer saying, "Dad, I need your help..." I just stared at him as he confessed and cried out to his Dad. I was a speechless onlooker of the Spirit mixing with a young soul, fathering my son, prompting him to cry out, "Abba!" Jeremy, you have stewarded Jackson well.

Made in the USA
Monee, IL
13 January 2025

76784301R00046